D1179319

This Father's Book is the property of the following father:

....

....

Any children caught stealing this book
from their dad will be disinherited
automatically.

At last, here is an antidote
to the mushy clichés that
surround parenthood: a practical
guidebook that tells it like it is.

Packed with useful tools and tips,
it's what every contemporary
father needs to make a success
of the fathering business.

Follow its advice, and
your darling children will
love and cherish you forever.
Ignore it, and they will
put you in a home.

Happy fathering!

PARENTAL LICENCE

This licence allows you to conceive and bring up children. It must be produced when required by Social Services, education authorities, the police, or other relevant government agencies.

IMPORTANT DOCUMENT! KEEP YOUR VALIDATED LICENCE IN A SAFE PLACE.

Name:

Address:

Date Of Birth:

Signature:

The above-named is licensed to father an unlimited number of children.

Photo

Official use only

SP ☐   PD ☐   Z ☐   Z+ ☐

Fail ☐   Pass ☐

Refer DHSS ☐   Refer DWP ☐

Refer Inland Revenue ☐

Refer NSPCC ☐   Refer RSPCA ☐

CHILDREN COVERED BY THIS LICENCE

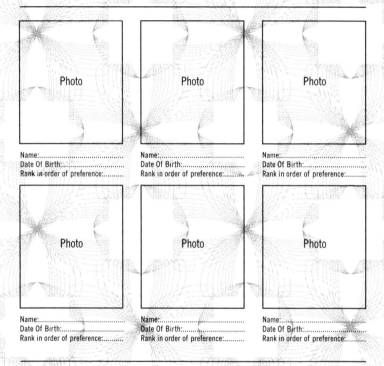

Photo

Name:......................................
Date Of Birth:.........................
Rank in order of preference:..........

Photo

Name:......................................
Date Of Birth:.........................
Rank in order of preference:..........

Photo

Name:......................................
Date Of Birth:.........................
Rank in order of preference:..........

Photo

Name:......................................
Date Of Birth:.........................
Rank in order of preference:..........

Photo

Name:......................................
Date Of Birth:.........................
Rank in order of preference:..........

Photo

Name:......................................
Date Of Birth:.........................
Rank in order of preference:..........

PENALTY POINTS: Should you commit a parenting offence, you will incur penalty points on your licence. More than 12 points may lead to disqualification from parenting and your children being taken into care. The following is a non-comprehensive guide to the number of points that may be imposed. Swearing in front of your child: 1 point. Letting child watch too much television: 2 points. Undermining other parent's authority: 3 points. Telling your child they were an accident: 5 points. Telling your child they were adopted (unless true): 6 points. Accidentally running over your child's pet: 7 points. Deliberately running over your child's pet: 9 points. Deliberately running over your child: licence withdrawn in perpetuity.

Children's Birthday Reminder

	Name
Child no.1	
Child no.2	
Child no.3	
Child no.4	
Child no.5	
Child no.6	
Child no.7	
Child no.8	
Child no.9	
Child no.10*	

Write down the names and dates of birth of
your children. Never forget a birthday again!

	Boy	Girl	Time and Circumstances of Conception	Date of Birth

*Vasectomy is not nearly as expensive or painful as people believe, you know.

Top 10 excuses for forgetting your child's birthday

I was following the Byzantine calendar.

Your mother lied to me about the date.

Actually, I have Alzheimer's.

I just celebrated your birthday in silence.

I didn't forget, it's just tough love.

I'm waiting for them to invent a good enough present.

I remembered last year.

I was kidnapped by anti-family protesters.

Fooled you, didn't I? Here's some money.

I thought we'd sent you to boarding school.

Choosing your child's career

Your children are your future. Here are some solid careers, along with subtle hints you may drop to steer your kids in the right direction.

1. Doctor
Money: *$$$*
Hint: *"Doctors save lives. And even when they don't, they still get paid!"*

2. Lawyer
Money: *$$$$*
Hint: *"Lawyers are very important, look how many TV shows they're in."*

3. Arms dealer
Money: *$$$$$*
Hint: *"Explosions are fun! Particularly in foreign countries."*

4. Teacher
Money: *$*
Hint: *"Well, at least you can't get fired."*

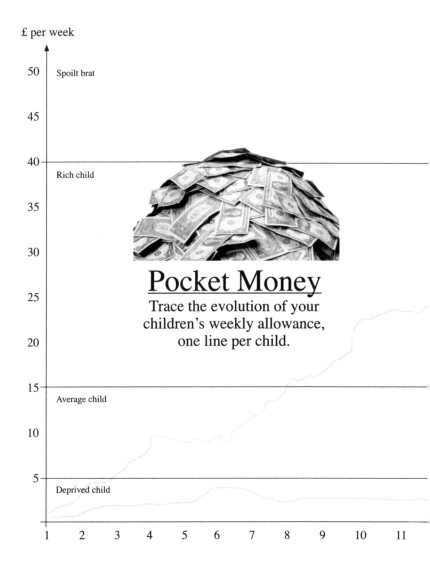

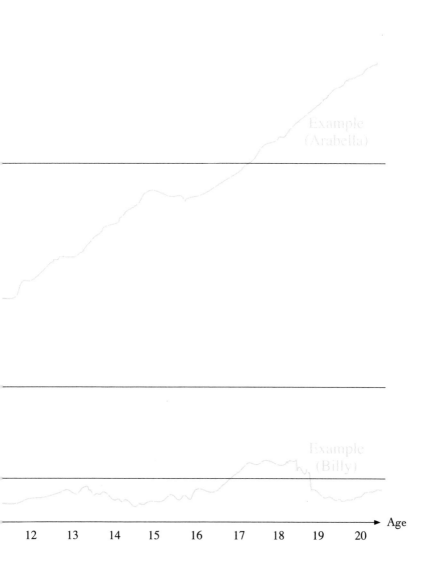

Example
(Arabella)

Example
(Billy)

Age

12   13   14   15   16   17   18   19   20

Role modelling

Pick the role model that you seek to embody as a father. Roles available:

Loving Father ☐
"Your hamster, Alfie, passed away, let's have a big hug for him in heaven"

Strict Father ☐
"You can bury your hamster when you've finished your homework"

Drunken Father ☐
"Ruddy hamster run under my bloody foot!? Not my fault hic"

Distant Father ☐
"I didn't know you
had a hamster? Anyway,
it died this morning"

Absent Father ☐
"Guy in the next cell
to mine kept one, until
the screws found it"

Evil Stepfather ☐
"Three guesses what
you just had for dinner!"

The facts of life: telling it straight

To avoid any psychological trauma in later life, this is how you should break the facts of life to your children. Follow this tried-and-tested script to the letter:

"Umm now look here, ^{Insert name of child}   ,
see, there's something your mother and I have
been meaning to talk to you about. Blimey
it's hot in here isn't it, yes, now, Mummy
and Daddy love you very much, and, well,
Mummy and Daddy love each other very much
too, and, so, remember how you came out of
Mummy's tummy, yes? Well, Daddy put you
there in the first place. How? Well! Help me out
here, ^{Insert name of wife}   , yes well, Daddy
used his ummm… doodah to fertilise Mummy,
like a beautiful flower, you see? No? OK. You
were inside Daddy and then Daddy put you
inside Mummy, like magic. No, no, scrap that:
Daddy put his ding-dong inside Mummy's
belly and moved it around a bit, and ta-dah you
were made! No it didn't hurt, did it Mummy?
But never mind that for now, where was I,
anyway that's pretty much it, good luck with it
someday, now what about a nice cup of tea?"

The recommended age for this conversation is 21.

<u>Newspeak</u>

Avoid teaching them these words
when they're very young, and save
yourself a lot of trouble later on:

Important: Make sure relatives, teachers and friends know not to use these words in front of your children, either.

~~Want~~

~~I~~

~~Me~~

~~Toy~~

Dancing in front of your children: *the rules*

1. Get drunk first.
Maximum embarrassment cannot be achieved sober.

2. Pick what you consider to be a "modern" dancing style.
Breakdancing is perfect.

3. Involve your child.
Shouting "yo" at them will make them feel included.

4. Involve your child's friends.
The other kids will praise your child for having such a groovy dad.

Baby Expenses

Date	Item	Expense
23/01/07	Cot	£ 239
24/01/07	Nappies	£ 18.99
04/02/07	Rattle	£ 6.99
28/02/07	Baby phone	£ 73
02/03/07	Buggy	£ 292
11/03/07	Talcum powder	£ 4
01/04/07	High chair	£ 109
15/04/07	Car seat	£ 144.80
		£
		£
		£
		£
		£
		£
		£
		£
		£
		£
	TOTAL:	£

By the time your child reaches adulthood, on average they will have cost you approximately £1,000,000. Keep tabs on the expenditure, and bill them at 18. ■ = Examples

Date	Item	Expense
		£
		£
		£
		£
		£
		£
		£
		£
		£
		£
		£
		£
		£
		£
		£
		£
		£
		£
	TOTAL:	£

Accounting note: Christmas- and birthday presents are not chargeable

Manly things to teach your son

Teach your boy the ins and outs of manhood!

BUILDING A TREEHOUSE
"The key to a top-notch treehouse lies in finding sturdy branches!"

THE ART OF SHAVING
"Wet your skin with warm water first, then shave downwards only!"

Art page: *Is your child the next Picasso?*

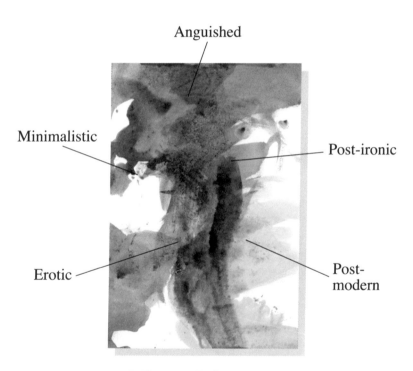

Anguished

Minimalistic

Post-ironic

Erotic

Post-modern

Next Picasso
Value: $2,000,000

Your child could well be a prodigy. Examine his or her scribblings carefully for signs of artistic genius, and bank the millions their work will sell for. Here is how to tell:

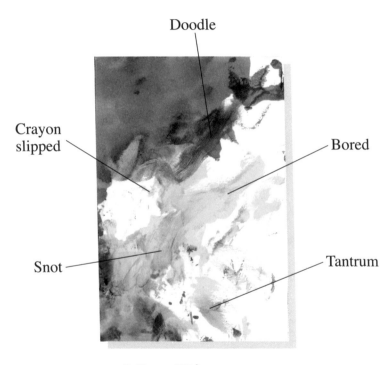

Doodle

Crayon slipped

Bored

Snot

Tantrum

Not Picasso
Value: $3

Gifts from your children

Ties	Date: 18/06/03 Occasion: Father's Day From: Lizzie Detail: Green silk with yellow dots	Date:............. Occasion:............. From:............. Detail:	Date:............. Occasion:............. From:............. Detail:	Date:............. Occasion:............. From:............. Detail: ....
Socks	Date: 25/12/06 Occasion: Christmas From: Milo Detail: Grey (50% lambswool)	Date:............. Occasion:............. From:............. Detail:	Date:............. Occasion:............. From:............. Detail:	Date:............. Occasion:............. From:............. Detail: ....
Shaving-related items	Date: 25/12/06 Occasion: Christmas From: Tommy Detail: Gillette "Travel Kit"	Date:............. Occasion:............. From:............. Detail:	Date:............. Occasion:............. From:............. Detail:	Date:............. Occasion:............. From:............. Detail: ....
Gadgets	Date: 22/04/07 Occasion: 50th birthday From: Milo Detail: Robot alarm clock	Date:............. Occasion:............. From:............. Detail:	Date:............. Occasion:............. From:............. Detail:	Date:............. Occasion:............. From:............. Detail: ....
Joke items	Date: 18/06/06 Occasion: Father's Day From: Bruce Detail: Beer-holding remote control	Date:............. Occasion:............. From:............. Detail:	Date:............. Occasion:............. From:............. Detail:	Date:............. Occasion:............. From:............. Detail: ....

The range of authorised gifts from children to fathers
is strictly limited, which makes it difficult for you to
remember who gave you what. Keep track here.

Date:......	Date:......	Date:......	Date:......	Date:......
Occasion:......	Occasion:......	Occasion:......	Occasion:......	Occasion:......
From:......	From:......	From:......	From:......	From:......
Detail:......	Detail:......	Detail:......	Detail:......	Detail:......
Date:......	Date:......	Date:......	Date:......	Date:......
Occasion:......	Occasion:......	Occasion:......	Occasion:......	Occasion:......
From:......	From:......	From:......	From:......	From:......
Detail:......	Detail:......	Detail:......	Detail:......	Detail:......
Date:......	Date:......	Date:......	Date:......	Date:......
Occasion:......	Occasion:......	Occasion:......	Occasion:......	Occasion:......
From:......	From:......	From:......	From:......	From:......
Detail:......	Detail:......	Detail:......	Detail:......	Detail:......
Date:......	Date:......	Date:......	Date:......	Date:......
Occasion:......	Occasion:......	Occasion:......	Occasion:......	Occasion:......
From:......	From:......	From:......	From:......	From:......
Detail:......	Detail:......	Detail:......	Detail:......	Detail:......
Date:......	Date:......	Date:......	Date:......	Date:......
Occasion:......	Occasion:......	Occasion:......	Occasion:......	Occasion:......
From:......	From:......	From:......	From:......	From:......
Detail:......	Detail:......	Detail:......	Detail:......	Detail:......

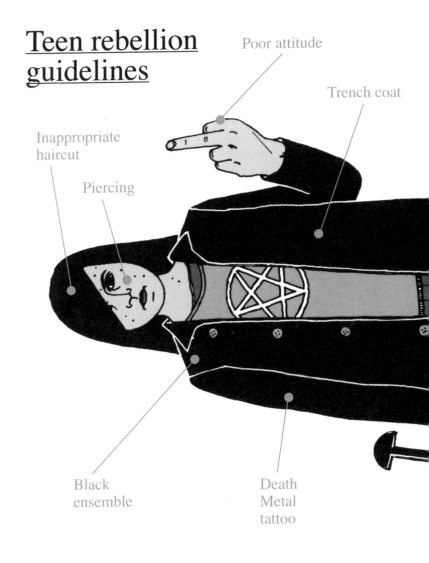

Teen rebellion guidelines

Poor attitude

Trench coat

Inappropriate haircut

Piercing

Black ensemble

Death Metal tattoo

Some degree of rebelliousness is pretty much compulsory for teenagers. But how can you tell if your teen is just going through a legitimate middle-class rebellious phase, or if they're actually planning to shoot up their whole school and land you in some potentially serious legal trouble? Middle-class rebellion = ■ Legal trouble = ■

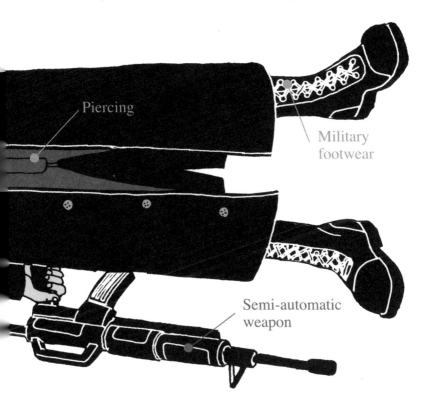

Piercing

Military footwear

Semi-automatic weapon

Piggybacking:
The Best Of

Every child has cherished memories
of their dad giving them a piggyback
ride. Make yours the most memorable
of all: here are the world's top rides.

Snowdon	Estimated time: *8 hours* View: Level of difficulty:

Great Wall of China (Heaven's Ladder)	Estimated time: *5 hours* View: Level of difficulty:

Himalayan foothills

Estimated time: *2 to 6 days*

View:

Level of difficulty:

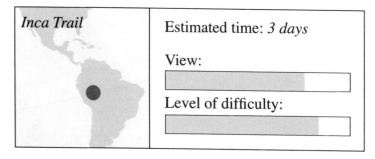

Inca Trail

Estimated time: *3 days*

View:

Level of difficulty:

Kilimanjaro

Estimated time: *6 days*

View:

Level of difficulty:

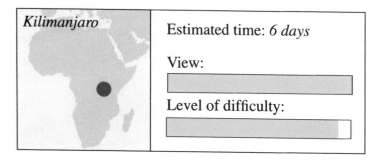

Taking your children to the office

It is important to expose your offspring to the world of work as early as possible. Involve them in your job, but remember to make it fun!

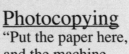

Photocopying
"Put the paper here, and the machine makes a paper baby!"

Filing
"Feed the cupboard monster, or he'll swallow you up!"

Message taking
"Santa's going to ring you any minute now, so make sure you pick up!"

Pay-rise negotiating
"Cry for ten minutes in front of Daddy's boss and get a shiny new Playstation for Christmas!"

Santa vs Osama: _Teaching your child the difference_

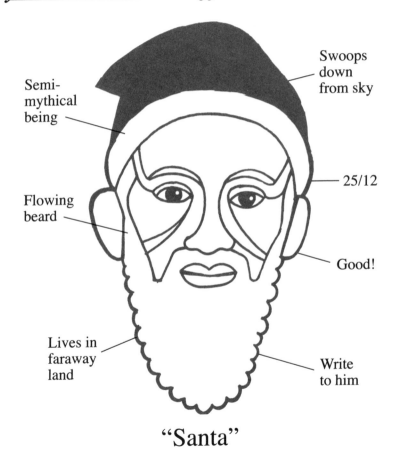

Semi-mythical being

Swoops down from sky

25/12

Flowing beard

Good!

Lives in faraway land

Write to him

"Santa"

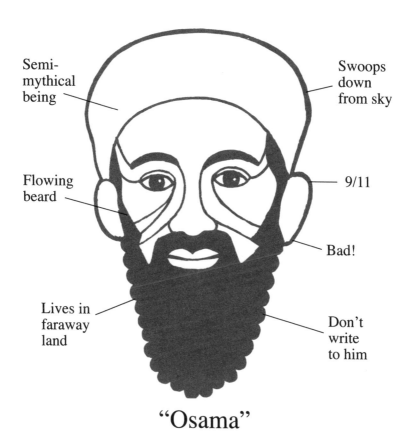

Semi-
mythical
being

Swoops
down
from sky

Flowing
beard

9/11

Bad!

Lives in
faraway
land

Don't
write
to him

"Osama"

Homework Cheat Sheet

Times Table

1	2	3	4	5	6	7	8	9	10	11	12	13	14	15
2	4	6	8	10	12	14	16	18	20	22	24	26	28	30
3	6	9	12	15	18	21	24	27	30	33	36	39	42	45
4	8	12	16	20	24	28	32	36	40	44	48	52	56	60
5	10	15	20	25	30	35	40	45	50	55	60	65	70	75
6	12	18	24	30	36	42	48	54	60	66	72	78	84	90
7	14	21	28	35	42	49	56	63	70	77	84	91	98	105
8	16	24	32	40	48	56	64	72	80	88	96	104	112	120
9	18	27	36	45	54	63	72	81	90	99	108	117	126	135
10	20	30	40	50	60	70	80	90	100	110	120	130	140	150
11	22	33	44	55	66	77	88	99	110	121	132	143	154	165
12	24	36	48	60	72	84	96	108	120	132	144	156	168	180
13	26	39	52	65	78	91	104	117	130	143	156	169	172	195

Pi

3.14159265358979323846264338327950288419716939937510582097494459230781640628620899862803482534211706798214808651328230664709384460955058223172535940812848111745028410270193852110555964462294895493038196442881097566593344612847564 82

Trigonometry

$\sin\theta$ = Opposite Side/Hypotenuse
$\cos\theta$ = Adjacent Side/Hypotenuse
$\tan\theta = \sin\theta/\cos\theta$ = Opposite Side/Adjacent Side
$\operatorname{cosec}\theta = 1/\sin\theta$ = Hypotenuse/Opposite Side
$\sec\theta = 1/\cos\theta$ = Hypotenuse/Adjacent Side
$\cot\theta = 1/\tan\theta = \cos\theta/\sin\theta$ = Adjacent Side/Opposite Side
$\sin\theta\operatorname{cosec}\theta = \cos\theta\sec\theta = \tan\theta\cot\theta = 1$
$\sin(90-\theta) = \cos\theta$, $\cos(90-\theta) = \sin\theta$
$\sin^2\theta + \cos^2\theta = 1$
$\tan^2\theta + 1 = \sec^2\theta$
$\cot^2\theta + 1 = \operatorname{cosec}^2\theta$
$\sin(A+B) = \sin A\cos B + \cos A\sin B$
$\sin(A-B) = \sin A\cos b - \cos A\sin B$
$\cos(A+B) = \cos A\cos B - \sin A\sin B$
$\cos(A-B) = \cos A\cos B + \sin A\sin B$
$\tan(A+B) = (\tan A + \tan B)/(1 - \tan A\tan B)$
$\tan(A-B) = (\tan A - \tan B)/(1 + \tan A\tan B)$
$\cot(A+B) = (\cot A\cot B - 1)/(\cot A + \cot B)$
$\cot(A-B) = (\cot A\cot B + 1)/(\cot B - \cot A)$
$\sin(A+B) + \sin(A-B) = 2\sin A\cos B$
$\sin(A+B) - \sin(A-B) = 2\cos A\sin B$
$\cos(A+B) + \cos(A-B) = 2\cos A\cos B$
$\cos(A-B) - \cos(A-B) = 2\sin A\sin B$
$\sin C + \sin D = 2\sin[(C+D)/2]\cos[(C-D)/2]$
$\sin C - \sin D = 2\cos[(C+D)/2]\sin[(C-D)/2]$
$\cos C + \cos D = 2\cos[(C+D)/2]\cos[(C-D)/2]$
$\cos C - \cos D = 2\sin[(C+D)/2]\sin[(D-C)/2]$

Latin Verbs

To be					
Indicative Mood					
Present	sum	es	est	sumus	estis	sunt
Imperfect	eram	eras	erat	eramus	eratis	erant
Future	ero	eris	erit	erimus	eritis	erunt
Perfect	fui	fuisti	fuit	fuimus	fuistis	fuerunt
Pluperfect	fueram	fueras	fuerat	fueramus	fueratis	fuerant
Future Perfect	fuero	fueris	fuerit	fuerimus	fueritis	fuerint
Subjunctive Mood					
Present	sim	sis	sit	simus	sitis	sint
Imperfect	essem	esses	esset	essemus	essetis	essent
Perfect	fuerim	fueris	fuerit	fuerimus	fueritis	fuerint
Pluperfect	fuissem	fuisses	fuisset	fuissemus	fuissetis	fuissent
Imperative Mood					
Present	—	es	—	—	este	—
Future	—	esto	esto	—	estote	sunto

As a father, you are expected to help your offspring with their homework. Here is a handy reminder of the things you are supposed to know off the top of your head. Refer to it discreetly to avoid sinking in your children's estimation.

Periodic Table

1 H																	2 He
3 Li	4 Be											5 B	6 C	7 N	8 O	9 F	10 Ne
11 Na	12 Mg											13 Al	14 Si	15 P	16 S	17 Cl	18 Ar
19 K	20 Ca	21 Sc	22 Ti	23 V	24 Cr	25 Mn	26 Fe	27 Co	28 Ni	29 Cu	30 Zn	31 Ga	32 Ge	33 As	34 Se	35 Br	36 Kr
37 Rb	38 Sr	39 Y	40 Zr	41 Nb	42 Mo	43 Tc	44 Ru	45 Rh	46 Pd	47 Ag	48 Cd	49 In	50 Sn	51 Sb	52 Te	53 I	54 Xe
55 Cs	56 Ba	57 La	72 Hf	73 Ta	74 W	75 Re	76 Os	77 Ir	78 Pt	79 Au	80 Hg	81 Tl	82 Pb	83 Bi	84 Po	85 At	86 Rn
87 Fr	88 Ra	89 Ac	104 Rf	105 Db	106 Sg	107 Bh	108 Hs	109 Mt	110 Uun	111 Uuu	112 Uub	113	114 Uuq				

58 Ce	59 Pr	60 Nd	61 Pm	62 Sm	63 Eu	64 Gd	65 Tb	66 Dy	67 Ho	68 Er	69 Tm	70 Yb	71 Lu
90 Th	91 Pa	92 U	93 Np	94 Pu	95 Am	96 Cm	97 Bk	98 Cf	99 Es	100 Fm	101 Md	102 No	103 Lr

Capital City & Population
Buenos Aires 39,537,943
La Paz 8,857,870
Brasilia 186,112,794
Santiago 16,136,137
Bogota 42,954,279
Quito 13,363,593
Cayenne 195,506
Georgetown 765,283
Asuncion 6,347,884
Lima 27,925,628
Paramaribo 438,144
Montevideo 3,415,920
Caracas 25,375,281

Roman Emperors

Augustus 27 BC– AD14	Didius Julianus 193	Florianus 276	Julian 360–363
Tiberius 14–37	Septimius Severus 193–211	Probus 276–282	Jovian 363–364
Caligula 37–41	Caracalla 211–217	Carus 282–283	Valentinian 364–375
Claudius 41–54	Macrinus 217–218	Numerian 283–284	Gratian 367–383
Nero 54–68	Elagabalus 218–222	Carinus 283–285	Valentinian II 375–392
Galba 68–69	Alexander Severus 222–235	Diocletian 284–305	Eugenius 392–394
Otho 69	Maximinus Thrax 235–238	Maximian 286–305	Honorius 395–423
Vitellius 69	Gordian III 238–244	Constantius I 305–306	John 423–425
Vespasian 69–79	Phillippus Arabs 244–249	Galerius 305–311	Valentinian III 425–455
Titus 79–81	Decius 249–251	Severus II 306–307	Petronius Maximus 455
Domitian 81–96	Trebonianus Gallus 251–253	Constantine 307–337	Avitus 455–456
Nerva 96–98	Aemilius Aemilianus 253	Maxentius 306–312	Majorian 457–461
Trajan 98–117	Valerian 253–260	Maximian 307–308	Severus III 461–465
Hadrian 117–138	Gallienus 253–268	Licinius 308–324	Anthemius 467–472
Antoninus Pius 138–161	Claudius II 268–270	Maximinus Daia 310–313	Alybrius 472
Marcus Aurelius 161–180	Quintillus 270	Constantine II 337–340	Glycerius 473–474
Commodus 180–192	Aurelian 270–275	Constans 337–350	Julius Nepos 474–475
Pertinax 193	Tacitus 275–276	Constantius II 337–361	Romulus Augustus 475–476

<u>Shaping your newborn's head</u>

Babies are born with malleable heads, as some of their skull bones don't solidify for months. Take advantage of this to mould their features into the most advantageous shape, by applying firm pressure at the points indicated twice a day for the first nine months.

1. High cheekbones are universally attractive
2. A high forehead conveys intelligence
3. Boys need a strong, masculine chin
4. An upturned nose looks cute on girls
5. Larger eyes are more attractive
6. A nice smile will help your child through life

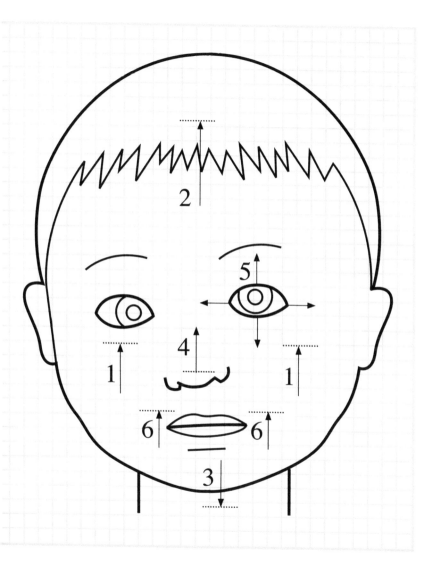

SPORT: finding the good in every child's performance

Tennis
"Hey, that was a really powerful serve! Now try again but hit the ball."

Football
"An own goal is still a goal! Well done!"

Swimming
"Life isn't about winning the race, it's about not drowning along the way."

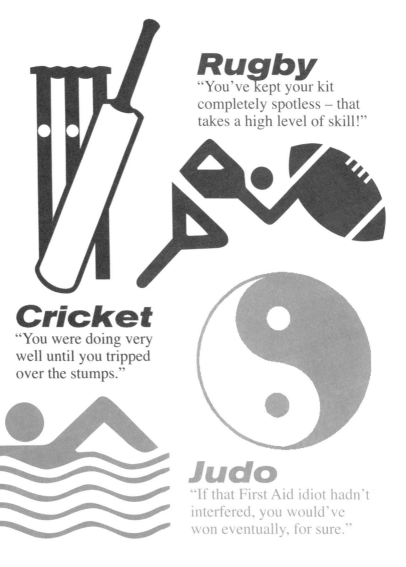

Rugby
"You've kept your kit completely spotless – that takes a high level of skill!"

Cricket
"You were doing very well until you tripped over the stumps."

Judo
"If that First Aid idiot hadn't interfered, you would've won eventually, for sure."

Surfing the net safely

The internet is fraught with dangers for your children. The only way to ensure they are safe is to join them online and keep an eye on their activities.

Register on MySpace yourself.

Give yourself a friendly profile name, like SmilyCindee!!

To blend in, claim to be the same age as your kids, e.g. 14.

Introduce yourself to the others. "Are your parents mean to you?" and "Where do you live?" are suitable opening gambits.

Monitor your kids' profiles and Friends List for suspicious goings-on.

Try to spot grown men impersonating kids and report them immediately.

Lifelong fathering

Fatherhood doesn't stop when your kids reach 18. You will need to step in throughout their lives to provide guidance and protection in delicate grown-up situations.

Professional situations:
"My girl just completed the Globocorp deal, so make her vice-president or I'll smack you one!"

Legal situations:
"You can release my son, your honour, I vouch for his innocence."

The 10 essential teachings that every parent must inculcate in their kids.

Test them at 18 before releasing them into the big wide world.

	(Tick)
1. Correct usage of toilet	☐
2. Holding of knife and fork	☐
3. Looking both ways before crossing the road	☐
4. Not accepting sweets from strangers	☐
5. Difference between good and evil	☐
6. It's not the winning, it's the taking part	☐
7. Crime doesn't pay	☐
8. Violence never solved anything	☐
9. Money can't buy you happiness	☐
10. Life is short and then you die (optional)	☐

Daddy's little helpers

Overuse of tranquillizers has historically been associated with motherhood. But as a new man and a modern, overworked father, you should pop them too. Here is a handy guide to some of the favourites, along with potential side-effects to look out for.

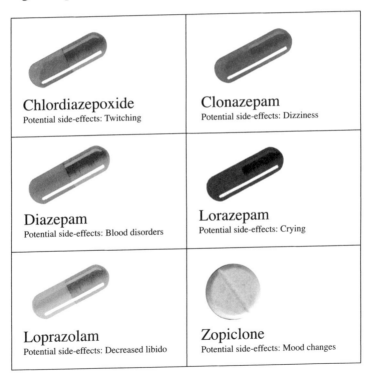

Chlordiazepoxide
Potential side-effects: Twitching

Clonazepam
Potential side-effects: Dizziness

Diazepam
Potential side-effects: Blood disorders

Lorazepam
Potential side-effects: Crying

Loprazolam
Potential side-effects: Decreased libido

Zopiclone
Potential side-effects: Mood changes

Nitrazepam
Potential side-effects: Amnesia

Lormetazepam
Potential side-effects: Shaky movements

Oxazepam
Potential side-effects: Hallucinations

Temazepam
Potential side-effects: Aggression

Zaleplon
Potential side-effects: Nausea

Zolpidem
Potential side-effects: "Drugged" feeling

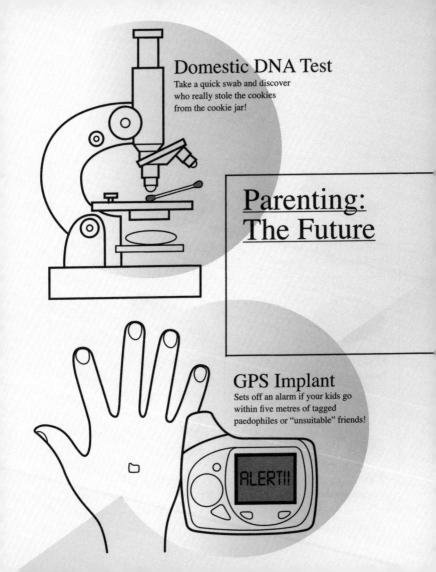

Domestic DNA Test

Take a quick swab and discover who really stole the cookies from the cookie jar!

Parenting: The Future

GPS Implant

Sets off an alarm if your kids go within five metres of tagged paedophiles or "unsuitable" friends!

ALERT!!

Prozac-flavoured Dummy

Puts your unhappy baby in a better mood in minutes!

Keep abreast of the latest trends in fatherhood here.

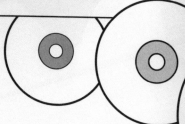

Subliminal Politics

Pass on your political beliefs to your kids painlessly in their sleep: choice of right-wing, left-wing, or centrist CDs!

Subtle ways in which your teenage children will let you know they love and appreciate you

Ignoring you in public

Ignoring you in private

Ridiculing you in public

Ridiculing you in private

Rejecting your career advice

Rejecting your career

Rejecting all you stand for

Giving you this book

FATHER

Fathers are encouraged to enter Benrik's new TV show, which sets out to find the world's daddiest dad! Coming soon!

TATTOO TOLERANCE Try staying calm as your 13-year-old shows off her new tattoo!

SANTA SURPRISE Dads battle it out to convince kids that they're the real Santa.

ULTIMATE COUCH POTATO Which dad can change channels quickest?

R IDOL

The Daddy of all Daddies!

ASBO ATTACK
You have five minutes to break up a group of teenage yobs!

DRIVING TEST
Teach the UK's clumsiest teen to drive!

"OOPS GRAN'S DROPPED THE BABY!"
Can you catch it in time?

TOP PRIZE!
The champion wins a cute Bulgarian nanny for a year!

To apply, visit www.thiswebsitewillchangeyourlife.com

Post-natal abortion:
Your Rights

The fact is not widely publicized, but you are
allowed to abort your offspring well after the statutory
24 weeks, indeed until the age of 18. We provide the
regulation form, which must be countersigned by
the child's mother. Consult your GP for details.

Form A-6734-009767

My dear child .... ,

Having you seemed like a good idea at the time,
but due to your recent bad behaviour / financial
difficulties / a change of mind on my part, I,
your father, have decided to exercise my right
to post-natal abortion. Please turn up at
.... Clinic on the
............/............/............ at .... (time)
for the simple and painless procedure. Goodbye,
and thank you for your time as my child.

Signed: .... (Daddy)

Countersigned by Mummy:
I agree with your father ....

Fatherhood Test
How good a father are you?

How many children do you have?
One...+3
More than one..+4
Paternity tests still pending..........................+1

How did you celebrate their birth?
Cutting umbilical cord....................................+5
Cutting Montecristo cigar...............................+4
Cutting and running.......................................+1

Which best describes your children?
Apple of your eye..+5
Light of your life...+6
Pain in your backside.....................................+1

To protect your little ones from harm, would you:

Run through fire...+4

Wrestle with sharks...+5

Rein in your drink-driving..+2

Overall, do your kids prefer you or their mother?

Me!...+4

Their mother...+3

Mother left long ago..+1

Results

Over 25 points: You are an exemplary father whose kids will grow up free of major mental trauma.

Between 15 and 25 points: You are a very good father – any problems your kids have must be due to their mum.

Under 15 points: Looking forward, please use adequate contraception.

If you liked The Father's Book, you'll love The Mother's Book!

Features:

- Deciphering teenspeak:
  a glossary
- Picking non-psychotic babysitters
- How to make children eat
  the uglier vegetables
- Criticizing other
  people's offspring
- Teenage rebellion:
  how to suppress it
- Kicking your older kids
  out of the nest
- Grey hairs: which child
  to blame most?

Benrik
Limited
presents:

THE

Mother's
BOOK

Every Mum's Essential Companion!

And if you are not on speaking terms with "the mother", just purchase
a copy and deduct the expense from your alimony payments.

Benrik Limited are Ben Carey and Henrik Delehag, authors of *This Diary Will Change Your Life* and *The Couple's Book*. Benrik specialize in "extreme self-help": their prescriptions will definitely change your life, but perhaps not for the better. Both would like to make clear that this book is not based on their personal experience growing up, nor does it reflect in any way on their parents' skills.

The right of Benrik Limited to be identified as the Author of the Work has been asserted in accordance with the Copyright, Designs and Patents Act 1988. All artwork by Benrik except as follows. Photography © Getty Images (Dollars by Steven Puetzer; Bird by Cyril Laubscher; Career kids 2, 3 and 4 by Taxi, Mark Heithoff, David Rosenberg; Office Worker by Ranald Mackechnie; Doctor by Science Faction), © 2007 JupiterImages Corporation (Career kid 1). Picasso Illustrations © Johanna Ehde.

First published 2007 by Boxtree
An imprint of Pan Macmillan Ltd
Pan Macmillan, 20 New Wharf Road, London N1 9RR
Basingstoke and Oxford
Associated companies throughout the world
www.panmacmillan.com

ISBN 978-0-7522-2628-6

9 8 7 6 5 4 3 2 1

A CIP catalogue record for this book is available from the British Library

Printed and bound in Belgium by Proost

Benrik
Your Values Are Our Toilet Paper